CORNISH
CHRISTMAS
RECIPES

★

CONTENTS

INTRODUCTION

Christmas is very definitely one of my favourite times of the year. The sounds and smells as I cook my way towards Christmas Day are just some of the treats of the time of year. As my family and I spend a huge amount of time around our kitchen table, we always have a second Christmas tree in the corner. I always feel watching the lights and decorations flicker together brings a heightened sense of excitement and makes for real magical moments around the table.

This selection of recipes are all family favourites. They are straightforward for all cooking abilities and while no special skills are needed, if you fancy a taste of Christmas at any time of year, choose a couple of recipes from this book.

Whenever you cook them I hope you and your family enjoy these recipes as much as my family and I do.

Tamar Swift

A few thoughts on food...

Herbs can be tricky at this time of year, as the garden and climate are not necessarily suited to a full range of plants in the ground. I try to have a bag or two of 'mixed herbs' in my fridge drawer all the time. Herbs always jazz-up a pot of food, and are a fantastic addition to every meal.

Oil is another tricky ingredient. My favourite oils are herb-flavoured and I buy these whenever I see one that looks interesting. Some of my recipes include sunflower oil as it's high in vitamin E but do feel free to use any oil you have – especially if you bought it on holiday somewhere gloriously hot!

Peppercorns are worth investing in! They last a long time and I find I get a lot of grinds for my money. As such, I always buy a coloured selection – pink, green, white and black. For simplicity, the recipes in this book list black pepper.

Pastry – or more accurately – whether to make or buy pastry, can be a contentious issue. I'm usually rushing from one place to another and as such, I buy pastry. I would therefore definitely encourage everyone except the keenest pastry-makers, to do likewise. I realise it may not be exactly the same as homemade but for me, it's absolutely perfect for my recipes!

Vegan recipes – while many of these recipes are not strictly vegan, they could become so by using vegan ingredients for example, plant or seed-based drink or no-milk, vegan cheese and plant-based, 'no meat' pieces.

STARTERS

AUBERGINE, FETA & PINE NUT PESTO PARCELS

serves 8

- 1 500g pre-rolled puff pastry sheet
- 1 quantity pine nut pesto* (see page 14)
- 2 large Pelagonia grilled aubergine slices in oil

- 8 small chargrilled aubergine slices in oil
- 8 tsp pesto
- 100g feta cheese – sliced into 8
- 50g mozzarella

*Note: to make the pine nut pesto follow the same recipe for Walnut Pesto (see page 14) using 25g of pine nuts rather than walnuts.

Lay the sheet of puff pastry out on the table-top and cut into eight equal rectangles. Using a sharp knife, score the top into a lattice pattern. Place each pastry onto a non-stick baking tray and cook at 350°F/180°C for approx. 12 minutes or until each is beautifully risen and brown on top. Place on a rack and leave to cool. I usually do this first thing in the morning and leave them on the side until later.

Drain the aubergines from their oil and lay them on kitchen paper. Slice the larger aubergines into lengths, aprrox. 3mm thick. Cut the smaller aubergines in half across the middle.

About 30 minutes before you wish to eat, use a sharp knife to cut off the top layer of each pastry. Gently set them aside – you don't want to damage them! Place 1 tsp of pesto onto the pastry bottom and gently spread out. Place a few slices of the larger aubergine on top, followed by two pieces of the smaller aubergine. Break the feta cheese into smaller pieces and add to the aubergines. Placing the pastry lid on top and scatter some mozzarella over the pastry lid. Carefully transfer your pastry parcels to a non-stick baking tray and gently warm them in the oven for 8 minutes at 300°F/150°C or until heated through.

Serve with a small salad and a robust dressing.

HOT HERBY CAMEMBERT
makes 2

- 1 large camembert per
  2 people
- 2 sprigs rosemary

- 4 sprigs thyme
- 1 sprig sage
- 1 tbsp dried cranberries

Remove the leaves from all of the herbs and discard the stalks. Slice the camembert in half across the middle; sprinkle the herbs across the cheese, the cranberries, add a good grind of sea salt and freshly ground black pepper and cover with the second half of cheese and place in a baking dish.

Alternatively, remove the leaves from all of the herbs and discard the stalks. Place the camembert in a baking dish and rough up the top skin with a knife. Sprinkle the herbs across the cheese, add the cranberries and gently push into them into the surface so they remain in place.

Cook the camembert for 25 minutes at 380°F/195°C or until bubbling. Serve immediately with bread and anything else you have in the fridge; a charcuterie selection would be perfect.

ROASTED RED & YELLOW PEPPER & PESTO CROSTINI

serves 12

For the pesto
- 60g basil leaves – discard the stalks
- 25g pine nuts
- approx. 200ml olive oil

For the crostini
- 2 large red peppers
- 2 large yellow peppers

- 3 tbsp olive oil
- 75g Parmigiano Reggiano cheese – grated
- 24 destoned olives
- 1 small baguette
- sea salt & freshly ground black pepper

Place the basil leaves and pine nuts into a food processor. Pulse until fairly well chopped. Now turn the food processor on fully and trickle in the olive oil. You are aiming for a paste rather than a sauce. Stop adding oil once the correct consistency has been reached. Cover with a little extra olive oil, and chill until ready to use.

Slice the peppers in half, de-seed the inside and discard the seeds. Lay each pepper on a baking tray lined with silicone paper. Bake on a high shelf in the oven at 380°F/195°C for 10 minutes or until the skins begin to blacken and blister. Remove from the oven and immediately place in a clean plastic food bag. Seal the bag and set aside until cool; this process allows the skins to loosen for easy peeling. Once cool enough to handle, open the bag and peel each half of pepper, discarding the skin. Slice the peppers and set aside.

Slice the baguette into at least 12 rounds. Lay the slices out over a large baking tray lined with silicone paper. Brush each bread slice with olive oil. Bake in the middle of the oven at 380°F/195°C for approximately 6 minutes or until toasted to a golden colour. Turn the toast over, brush the second side with olive oil and toast as before. Remove and allow to cool.

When you're ready to assemble the crostini, lay the toasted baguette rounds on a non-stick baking tray. Top each slice with a generous teaspoonful of pesto and spread out. Divide the pepper over the slices of baguette, add the grated Parmigiano Reggiano and two olives to each crostini. Season and place in the oven for 12 minutes at 380°F/195°C or until the cheese is melted. Serve immediately.

SAUSAGES WITH HONEY & MUSTARD

serves 6

- 24 cocktail sausage
- 3 tbsp clear pouring honey
- 3 tbsp wholegrain mustard

Separate the sausages and prick each one with a knife. Combine the honey and mustard in a bowl, add the sausages and mix well.

Place in a non-stick oven dish and cook for 18 minutes at 380°F/195°C, shaking well at least half-way through to make sure they don't stick to the base. Serve with cocktail sticks.

If you wish to use large sausages, substitute the cocktail sausages for 18 large sausages, allowing three per person and therefore this recipe will serve 6.

MAIN
COURSES

CRISPY WALNUT PESTO & HERB COD

serves 4

For the walnut pesto
- 60g basil leaves – discard the stalks
- 25g walnut pieces
- approx. 200ml olive oil

For the fish
- 4 180g cod fillet steaks
- 160g breadcrumbs
- 100g fresh mixed herbs – finely chopped
- sea salt & freshly ground black pepper

Place the basil leaves and walnut pieces (bashed with a rolling pin if they're quite big) into a food processor. Pulse until fairly well chopped. Now turn the food processor on fully and trickle in the olive oil. You are aiming for a paste rather than a sauce. Stop adding oil once the correct consistency has been reached.

Mix the breadcrumbs and herbs together. Place the cod on a board and season well. Divide the pesto into four portions and spread along the length of each cod steak. Cover with the breadcrumbs and herb mixture and press down firmly to stick to the pesto. Using a pallet knife, transfer each steak carefully to a baking tray. Scoop on any breadcrumbs which fall off.

Cook in the oven for 25 minutes at 380°F/195°C or until cooked through and crispy on top.

Serve with a collection of new potatoes and small vegetables – French beans, mange tout and Chantenay carrots work particularly well.

DUCK WITH KEA PLUM SAUCE

serves 4

- 4 duck breasts
- 300ml red wine
- 1 tbsp Kea Plum jam

- sea salt & freshly ground black pepper

Place a frying pan over a high heat to bring it up to temperature. Don't add any oil. Prepare the duck breast by grinding sea salt and pepper over the skin. When the pan is hot, place each duck breast in, skin side down and keep it moving using a wooden spoon or large fork. When the oil begins to run from the duck skin you can allow it to sit without moving until the skin is browned. This usually takes about 4 minutes. At this point, turn the duck breast over, keep it moving for a few moments and then allow it to brown. Turn the heat down slightly if necessary.

When both sides are beautifully bronzed, turn up the heat and add the red wine. The juices in the pan may splatter so take care and wear oven gloves to cover your hands and arms. Now, either reduce the heat or, depending on your oven, place the pan in the oven for approximately 8 minutes at 350°F/180°C until the sauce has thickened slightly. Do keep an eye on the pan as you don't want the sauce to evaporate. Remove from the heat or oven and check the meat is cooked; the inside should register 325°F/170°C – check with a meat thermometer to be sure.

Place the duck breast in a warmed serving dish and set aside to relax. Return the sauce to a low heat and stir through the Kea Plum jam. Adjust the seasoning if desired.

Serve with chips and a light salad with the sauce on the side.

HAKE & MUSHROOM EN CROUTE

serves 4

- 4 160g hake steaks – without skin
- 4 large sprigs of fresh sage – stalk & leaves
- 1 500g pack puff pastry
- a little egg and milk

For the mushroom duxelles
- 25g butter
- 100g leek – finely chopped
- 2 cloves garlic – peeled and finely chopped
- 300g mushrooms – wiped & finely chopped
- 2 tbsp brandy or Madeira
- 1 tbsp fresh thyme leaves – chopped
- sea salt & freshly ground black pepper

Melt the butter over a medium heat and add the garlic. Gently fry for a few minutes before adding the leeks and continuing to cook; you are waiting for the leeks to soften slightly. Add the mushrooms, stir well and cook until the liquid has almost disappeared. Now add the brandy or Madeira and continue cooking to burn off the alcohol. You really want the flavour of the brandy or Madeira to come through without the sharpness of the alcohol.

When cooked, season well, stir in the thyme and cool. Refrigerate until needed.

HOMEMADE CHRISTMAS PASTY

serves 4

- 340g beef skirt
- 160g potatoes – diced
- 120g swede – diced
- 1 onion – chopped
- 500g shortcrust pastry
- sea salt & freshly ground black pepper

- 3 tbsp cold water
- 2 tbsp cranberry sauce (optional)
- milk/egg to glaze if required

In a bowl mix together the beef skirt, potato, swede and onion (and cranberry sauce if using). Add 3 tbsp of cold water and stir well. Season well and set aside. Roll out the pastry to about 4mm thick. Cut into rounds, using a saucer or a small plate.

Place some of this filling on one half of each circle of pastry, dampen the edges of the latter with the remaining cold water and fold the pastry over to cover the mixture.

Press the edges of the pastry together and crimp it with your fingers to seal. Make two or three ventilating slits in the 'lid', brush with beaten egg or milk if a glaze is required, and place on a baking tray.

Cook at 400°F/200°C for around 10 minutes until the pastry is pale brown, then reduce the heat to 375°F/190°C for about 40 minutes or until cooked through.

RED PEPPER, SPINACH & FETA MUFFINS

makes 10 - 12

- 2 large eggs – beaten
- 225g self-raising flour
- 20ml butter
- 70ml oil
- 50-100ml whole milk
- 1 roasted red pepper – finely chopped
- 10 olives – finely chopped
- 100g Stilton/feta cheese – grated/crumbled
- a little extra cheese for sprinkling
- sea salt & freshly ground black pepper

You will need a non-stick muffin tin.

Crack the eggs into a jug, pour in the oil and add enough milk to make 300ml. Season. Lightly stir through the red pepper followed by the Stilton cheese.

Pour the batter into the muffin cases and bake at 360°F/185°C for 20 - 30 minutes or until cooked. The muffins should rise, be firm to the touch and golden all over. An inserted skewer should come out clean.

Serve warm with a glass of prosecco!

ROASTED SALMON & PEPPERS

serves 4

- 4 200g salmon portions
- I small yellow pepper
- I small red pepper
- I small green pepper
- I shallot
- 4 sprigs thyme

For the marinade

- 4 tbsp olive oil
- I lemon – juiced
- I tbsp balsamic vinegar
- I tsp English mustard
- sea salt & freshly ground black pepper

Y ou will need 4 pieces of tin foil large enough to make parcels with the salmon and peppers inside.

Begin by washing the salmon thoroughly and removing any loose scales or bones. Dry carefully on paper towel.

Mix the olive oil, lemon juice, balsamic vinegar and English mustard together in a jug. Season well and set aside.

De-seed the peppers and cut them into slices approximately 15mm wide and mix together with the finely sliced shallot.

Lay out the foil; in the centre of each piece, place a piece of salmon. Divide the pepper and shallots equally on top of each piece of salmon. Now fold the foil up into parcels, sealing one end and leaving the other end open. Gently hold each parcel with one hand and with the other, pour in a quarter of the marinade. Carefully seal the second end of each parcel, making sure none of the juices escape. Allow the parcels to rest in the fridge for at least 20 minutes, longer if possible.

When you're ready to cook, place the parcels on a baking sheet and bake at 380°F/195°C for 25 minutes or until the parcels are puffed up and looking as though they are about to burst. Alternatively, place them on the hottest part of the barbeque and cook as before.

I serve these parcels on the table for everyone to open themselves. You will probably need to provide a dish for the used foil to go on to. The salmon should fall away from the skin when a knife is inserted through the fish.

Note: the parcels may be made up to 6 hours before they are needed, although they must be kept refrigerated until ready for cooking.

Serve with a green salad and new potatoes for a real taste of summer at Christmastime.

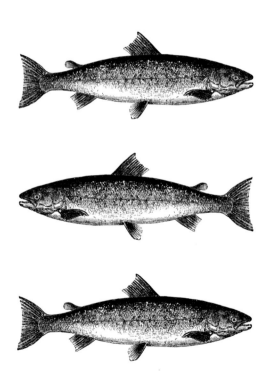

TRADITIONAL STARGAZEY PIE

serves 4

- 500g pack pastry – shortcrust or flaky
- 4 extra large eggs
- 4 rashers streaky bacon
- 50g leek
- 50g butter

- 1 lemon
- 3 tbsp parsley – chopped
- sea salt & freshly ground black pepper
- 8 pilchards

D ivide the pastry into $^1/_3$ and $^2/_3$, rolling out the $^2/_3$ and lining the base and sides of a deep-sided pie dish. Softly boil the eggs before peeling and cutting them in half. Prepare the pilchards by gutting, boning, washing and drying them carefully. Chop the bacon and leek into small slices before lightly frying in the butter.

Spread the bacon and leek over the base of the dish.

There are now two ways of finishing the pie. Arrange the pilchards around the edge of the dish, each with their head sticking over the side. Tuck the eggs in-between each fish and squeeze the lemon juice over. Roll out the pastry and cover the body of the fish, crimping the pastry neatly at the edges. Brush with a mixture of milk and egg for a shiny glaze.

Alternatively, arrange the eggs on top of the leek and bacon mixture, squeeze the lemon juice over and cover everything with the remaining pastry. Crimp the edges. Carefully cut a large cross in the centre of the pastry and peel it back before pushing each pilchard's tail into the dish and underneath the pastry, leaving the head sticking out. Fold the pastry back and tuck around the fish. Brush with a mixture of milk and egg for a shiny glaze.

Cook at 400°F/200°C for around 20 minutes or until the fish is cooked and the pastry golden.

STAR-GAZEY PIE
serves 4

- 8 pilchards or 12 good sized sardines
- 8 rashers streaky bacon
- 1 large onion – peeled & chopped
- 2 tsp fresh parsley – chopped
- sea salt & freshly ground black pepper
- 350g shortcrust pastry
- a little milk

This second Star-Gazey Pie is an alternative to the traditional recipe, presented slightly differently.

Gut, clean and bone the pilchards, leaving the heads in place. Wash thoroughly under cold water. Pat dry on kitchen paper before seasoning the inside with salt and pepper. Mix together the onion and parsley; stuff this mixture inside your pilchards. Roll out half of the pastry and line your baking dish. De-rind the streaky bacon, chop into small pieces and scatter over the base of your pastry in the pie dish. Brush the pastry rim with milk, then lay the fish on top of the bacon, cut sides down and with the heads on the rim. Sprinkle over any remaining onion and parsley mixture.

Roll out the remaining pastry. Brush the rim of the pastry dish with milk and cover the pie with your rolled-out pastry, pressing it down firmly around the fish heads. Brush the pastry lid with milk and bake in a pre-heated oven for 15 minutes at 375°F/190°C then reduce the heat to 350°F/180°C for a further 30 minutes. Do keep an eye on your pastry; you want it to be cooked and golden brown.

TOAD IN THE HOLE

serves 4

- 12 or 16 large pork & herb sausages depending on how hungry your guests are
- Sunflower oil – to coat the base of the cooking dish
- 3 extra large eggs
- 225g plain flour

- 225ml milk
- 165ml cold water
- 2 tbsp dried sage (optional)
- sea salt & freshly ground black pepper
- a few sprigs of rosemary – for serving

You will need a cooking dish large enough to lay the sausages out in a single layer and deep enough to allow your batter to double in size.

Separate the sausages and lay them over the base of the dish. Prick each sausage a couple of times. Pour over sufficient oil to come half-way up the side of each sausage – this may be quite a lot depending on how big your sausages are.

Break the eggs into a large mixing bowl. Using an electric hand whisk, initially on a low speed, slowly add the flour (and dried sage if using) until it is all whisked in to form a smooth paste. Combine the milk and water in a jug and again on a low speed, slowly add the liquid to the egg/flour, mixing well to ensure a smooth batter. Once you have added all the liquid, season the batter and have a final quick whisk. Pour the batter into a jug, making sure to include every last drop!

Place your sausages and oil in the oven at 380°F/195°C occasionally stirring the sausages to make sure they don't stick. When the oil is smoking hot, add the batter and return the pan to the oven. Cook for approximately 25 minutes or until the batter is risen, golden brown and a skewer inserted into the middle comes out clean. You may need to turn the dish around to ensure even cooking. Whatever you do though, don't open the oven door for at least 14 minutes.

Opening the door can cause the batter – your hole – to collapse. Wait until the batter looks risen either through the glass door or by opening the door very slightly and peeping in.

When cooked, decorate with your sprigs of rosemary and serve immediately. Toad in the Hole doesn't wait for anyone! I like to serve carrots, cauliflower and leeks with my Toad in the Hole. No potatoes though – the hole is more than enough!

WINTER CRANBERRY &
VEGETABLE CHICKEN

serves 4

- 4 large chicken breasts – skin on
- 1 large red onion
- 1 large sweet potato
- 1 small cauliflower
- 2 medium parsnips

For the marinade

- 3 tbsp cranberry sauce
- 2 tbsp olive oil
- 1 lime – juiced
- 1 tbsp roasted spice blend (Pul biber, sumac, garam masala)
- sea salt & freshly ground black pepper

Make a couple of slices across the skin of each chicken breast. Peel the vegetables and cut into large chunks, approximately 20mm each. Place all the marinade ingredients in a large bowl and whisk well. Add the vegetables and stir well – you may find it easier to use your hands! Now add the chicken and again stir well, coating everything in the marinade.

Transfer the chicken and vegetables to an oven proof dish, making sure the chicken is skin side up. Use a spatula to scoop all the lovely marinade into the cooking dish. Cover and refrigerate to allow the flavours to develop until you are ready to cook.

Place the chicken in a hot oven at 400°F/200°C for 10 minutes before reducing the heat to 375°F/190°C for 30 minutes or until the chicken is cooked. To test, carefully cut into one of the breasts across the middle; the flesh should be white with no pink showing. If necessary, return the chicken to the oven until completely cooked through.

Serve with cous cous which has had a 1 tbsp of freshly chopped parsley, thyme and chives stirred through it. Delicious!

BAKING

CHRISTMAS CAKE

serves 8-10

- 450g sultanas
- 450g currants
- 112g raisins
- 112g dates – lightly chopped
- 110g glacé cherries – chopped
- 50g mixed peel
- 1 lemon* – grated and juiced
- 1 orange* – grated and juiced
- 275g butter
- 275g caster sugar
- 6 eggs – lightly beaten
- 1 tbsp golden syrup
- 112g mixed spice
- 350g self-raising flour – sifted
- pinch of salt

Gather the dried fruit (sultanas, currants, raisins, dates, cherries and mixed peel) in a large mixing bowl. Mix them together before adding the rind and juice of the lemon and orange and again, stir well. Cover and leave in a cool (but not cold) place overnight.

Double line a 25cm cake tin with baking parchment. In addition to lining the tin, I always tie a double sheet of brown paper around the outside of the tin as this stops the cake drying-out whilst cooking. Prepare two circles of baking parchment for the top of the cake, each one with a hole cut in the middle to let the hot air escape.

Cream the butter and sugar together. Add the beaten eggs, one at a time (don't worry if it curdles) and then add the remaining ingredients, including your now-blossoming fruit. Finally, gently fold in the sifted flour (with the salt) so as not to lose any air. Place the mixture in the tin, flatten gently and cover the top with your baking parchment circles. Cook for 2 hours at 350°F/180°C and then reduce the oven to 300°F/150°C for a further 1 - 1½ hours. Test with a skewer to see if it's cooked. Allow to cool completely before removing it from the tin.

Remember to feed the cake once a week between making and icing, and keep the cake well sealed in an air-tight container.

Note: 'feeding' a cake is done by making six small holes in the top of the cake using a skewer. Carefully spoon in 1 tsp of orange juice, port or brandy, making sure the cake absorbs it before re-wrapping and sealing it in an air-tight container.

About a week before Christmas, cover the top and sides with marzipan and royal icing.

*The lemon and orange could be substituted for a wine-glass full of port or brandy or any other alcohol of your choice. Don't be afraid to use wine or cider – make your own tradition or try a different one each year. Variety is always a good idea!

JEWELLED BISCUITS

makes 12 jewels!

- 200g butter
- 100g soft brown sugar
- 300g plain flour

- pinch of salt
- 12 boiled sweets – various colours

If you are hanging these from the tree, you may wish to use 12 small cellophane bags each with a length of natural raffia ribbon.

Line a baking tray with silicone paper.

Place all the ingredients into the bowl of a food processor and pulse until it forms a ball. Gently roll the dough out and cut into shapes of your choice – stars, angels, bells, trees or a mixture of all!

Using a mini cutter or a sharp knife, cut out the same shape from the middle. Transfer to a baking tray. Place a boiled sweet in your cut-out, sprinkle with a little extra sugar and chill for at least 20 minutes.

Cook at 360°F/185°C for 25 minutes or until the biscuits are lightly golden and the boiled sweet has melted into the shortbread. Remove the biscuits from the oven and leave on the tray until completely cold.

Place one biscuit in each bag and tie with raffia ribbon. Hang from the tree or your suspended branch and allow eaters to choose their colour! Serve with hot chocolate for an extra treat!

Note: cook your 'removed' mini shapes at 360°F/185°C for 6-8 minutes or until lightly browned. When cool, ice each biscuit with icing made from 25g icing sugar and enough hot water to mix. Top each mini biscuit with a smartie and leave to set.

LAUNCESTON CAKE
serves 8-10

- 175g sugar
- 175g butter
- ½ tbsp black treacle
- 1 tbsp golden syrup
- 3 eggs

- 225g flour
- 50g ground almonds
- 450g currants
- 50g lemon peel

Cream the sugar and fat, add the treacle, syrup and then the eggs one at a time, beating each one in thoroughly before adding the next. Mix together the flour, almonds, currants and lemon peel, and fold them carefully into the mixture. Spoon into an 18cm tin and bake at 350°F/180°C for about 90 minutes or until cooked.

SALTED CARAMEL SHORTIES

makes 18

For the caramel
- 75g golden caster sugar
- 15g Cornish sea salt flakes

For the shortbread
- 125g plain flour
- 75g soft brown sugar
- 110g butter

Line two trays with baking parchment or use the same one twice.

For the caramel: gently heat the sugar until melted in a heavy-based saucepan, stirring frequently and making sure it doesn't 'catch' and burn. Continue heating gently until the sugar takes on a dark, glossy colour and texture. At this point, remove it from the heat, add the salt flakes and give a final stir. Now pour this sugar and salt mixture onto the lined tray, tilt to make sure it reaches all the corners and leave it to set.

Once completely cold, break the caramel into small pieces and set aside.

Note: care must be taken when heating sugar as it boils at a far higher temperature (around 320°F/160°C) than water (200°F/100°C) and can spit.

For the shortbread: sift the flour and sugar together into a bowl and rub in the butter. Gently knead in the caramel pieces until they are evenly distributed. Turn the caramel dough onto a floured board and divide into 18 pieces. Roll each piece into a ball, place them onto the baking parchment and flatten slightly.

Bake for 15 minutes at 350-375°F/180-190°C. Leave to cool.

PUDDING

BLACKCURRANT TRIFLE

serves 6

For the sponge
- 50g butter
- 50g caster sugar
- 50g self-raising flour
- 1 tsp baking powder
- 1 large egg
- 1 tbsp milk

For the trifle
- 580g tins blackcurrants
- 1 135g pack blackcurrant jelly
- 2 tbsp blackcurrant jam
- 1 pint Bird's custard – cooled
- 300ml double cream
- 1 Cadbury's Flake bar
- 12 silver cake decorating balls

Make the sponge by combining all the ingredients in a bowl and beating well for 2 minutes. Transfer to a cake tin and cook for approximately 14 minutes at 380°F/195°C or until the centre is springy and a skewer comes out clean. Set aside until cold.

Drain the blackcurrants, keeping the fruit juice for the jelly. Make the jelly as per the instructions on the packet using the blackcurrant juice as the liquid.

Slice the cake into appropriate sizes to line the base of your serving dish. I use a 240mm glass one I found in a charity shop. Spread jam on each piece of cake before you place it in the bowl. Snuggle the cake into the base to get a good covering. Now scatter the blackcurrants over the sponge and jam. Pour the jelly over everything, cover with cling film and refrigerate until fully set.

Make the custard as per the instructions on the pack. I use Bird's Custard Powder – the only kind of custard as far as my children are concerned. When the jelly is completely set, pour the cooled custard over, cover again and return to the fridge to set fully.

When the custard is set, whip the cream until just beginning to firm up. Spread over the custard and swirl the top. Keep the flake in its unopened packet and gently bash it with the back of a wooden spoon. When it feels as though it's roughly broken up, cut off the top corner and sprinkle straight from the packaging all over the cream. Drop 12 or so silver balls over the cream and flake and chill before serving.

Note: if your family prefer orange or strawberry jelly, simply use this with the appropriate tins of fruit. If you'd prefer a 1970's vibe, cover the top with coloured sprinkles – *Hundreds and Thousands* as they're called in the UK or *'love pearls'* elsewhere.

CHOCOLATE & GINGER ROULADE

serves 6

- 6 extra large eggs – separated
- 150g caster sugar + an extra 2 tbsp
- 45g cocoa powder
- 1 tsp brandy extract (optional)

- 400ml double cream
- 25g icing sugar
- 50g or 1 stem ginger – finely chopped

Y ou will need a Swiss roll tin or baking tray lined with silicone paper. Cut the paper into each corner to make sure it sits easily in the tin. Leave a good paper overhang for the Swiss roll to rise inside.

Begin by whisking the egg yolks and sugar together over a bowl of barely simmering water. Keep whisking until the mixture has at least doubled in size and leaves a strong 'ribbon' in the bowl when you lift the whisk and trail it across the mixture. Gently fold in the cocoa powder and brandy extract and set aside while you whisk the egg whites.

With completely clean whisks and bowl, whisk the egg whites to stiff peak stage – when they stand up in peaks and, if you invert the bowl, the egg whites remain in place. Fold the egg whites into the egg yolk and chocolate mixture, folding deftly but carefully without removing the air you've just whisked into your whites. Spread into the Swiss roll tin, tilting the tin to make sure the mixture reaches all four corners. Cook for approximately 20 minutes at 350°F/180°C or until the centre is springy to the touch and an inserted skewer comes out clean.

On a damp tea towel, lay out a piece of silicone paper with 2 tbsp caster sugar scattered over it. Once cooked, turn the roulade out onto the paper and caster sugar; peel off the silicone paper. At the short end nearest to you and using a sharp knife, cut a line half-way through the Swiss roll and all along the tea towel edge leaving about 10mm at each end. Fold this cut over and use the silicone paper to roll the roulade into. Be firm but not rough and the roulade should roll beautifully. Leave until cold before filling.

Whisk the double cream and icing sugar together until it begins to hold its shape. At this point add the stem ginger and stir gently. Open out the roulade and carefully spread the cream over the inside, leaving a 20mm cream-free space around all the edges. Roll up and transfer to a serving tray. Either sprinkle more caster sugar over or dredge the roulade in icing sugar and serve.

For real chocolate lovers, you could melt some chocolate in a bowl over barely simmering water and using a small jug or even a spoon, drizzle the chocolate in a zig-zag pattern along the top of the roulade. Chill until ready to serve.

CHRISTMAS PAVLOVA

serves 6

For the meringue
- 6 large egg whites
- 350g (golden) caster sugar

For the topping
- 600ml double cream
- 25g icing sugar (optional)
- 225g blackberries
- 150g blueberries
- 450g raspberries
- 400g strawberries
- 3 sprigs mint

Cut a piece of silicone paper large enough to fit on a baking tray. Draw a 250mm circle on it (I draw around a large dinner plate), turn the silicone paper over and place it with the drawn circle facing the tray but with the outline showing through.

Good meringues require a sparklingly clean whisk and bowl. Begin by placing the egg whites in the bowl and whisking until stiff peak stage. This is when the egg whites will stand up on their own and if you tilt the bowl, the whole mixture remains in place. When you have this stage, add the sugar one dessertspoon at a time, whisking thoroughly in between each addition. The aim is to achieve a smooth, glossy consistency by the time you've added and whisked in all the sugar.

If you add the sugar too quickly, the meringue will taste fine but it won't have the glorious sheen you really want and it will be brittle to touch. When you've whisked all the sugar into the egg whites, and achieved the glossy sheen and consistency, the mixture should remain exactly where it is if you turn the bowl upside down. If the mixture slips at all, keep whisking.

Spread the mixture onto your silicone paper, spreading it out to the edge of the circle you've drawn. You don't need to be too exact with the shaping. Try to keep the meringue to an even depth throughout. Swirl to finish.

Place the meringue in the oven for 12 minutes at 320°F/160°C before reducing the temperature to 300°F/150°C (depending on your oven) for at least an hour or until the meringue is completely firm throughout and comes off the paper easily. At this point, turn the oven off and leave until completely cold.

When cold, carefully lift the meringue and remove the paper. Place the meringue on your serving plate.

Wash and dry the fruit and sprigs of mint. I lay washed fruit on paper towels and pat them dry. Whisk the cream (and icing sugar if using) until it begins to hold its shape. Spread across the meringue, swirling to finish. Pile the fruit all over the cream, scattering the colours and finishing with a slightly raised centre. Tuck the sprigs of mint around the fruit and chill before serving.

A glass of chilled sparkling wine goes so well with this pudding; it is a favourite in our household for after midnight on New Year's Eve.

SECRET FUDGE PUDDING

serves 4

For the pudding
- 100g butter
- 100g caster sugar
- 2 large eggs
- 2 tbsp milk
- 35g self-raising flour

- 25g cocoa powder
- 1tsp baking powder

For the sauce
- 100g soft brown sugar
- 2 tbsp cocoa powder
- 300ml hot milk

You will need a buttered pudding bowl measuring 180mm.

Either place all the pudding ingredients into a bowl and whisk for 2 minutes until combined. Or, alternatively, cream the butter and sugar together until light and fluffy. Slowly add the egg and milk mixture, whisking well between each addition. Carefully fold in the sifted flour, cocoa and baking powder until combined. Transfer to the pudding bowl.

Place the sugar and cocoa powder into a bowl and pour on the hot milk, whisking all the time. Pour this over the pudding (yes, really) and bake at 375°F/190°C for approximately 40 minutes. The delicious chocolate sauce is hidden underneath the sponge – hence its secret name!

DRINKS

CHRISTMAS CRUSH

serves 6

- 1 lemon – grated & juiced
- 1 orange
- 200g caster sugar
- 600ml water
- 1 tsp ground ginger
- 1 bag of mulled wine spices

For serving
- a shot of gin or vodka for each glass (optional)
- slice of lime for each glass
- ½ cucumber
- a few fresh cranberries

Finely grate and juice the lemon and orange and mix them together. Dissolve the sugar in 200ml of the water which has been brought to the boil. Add the remaining cold water along with the fruit rind and juice, the ginger and mulled wine spice bag. Stir well and chill.

To serve, wash and dry the cranberries. Cut the lime into wedges and slice the cucumber in half lengthways and cut into thinner slices cross-wise. Line up your high-ball glasses, add some ice to each glass and pour in the gin or vodka if using. Add one or two cranberries, a couple of slices of cucumber and a wedge of lemon into each glass before topping up with the chilled Christmas crush. Stir well with a long spoon and serve.

CHRISTMAS SPRUCE

serves 6

- 1 lemon – scrubbed, peeled & juiced
- 350g granulated sugar
- 575ml boiling water
- 4 litres very cold water
- 2 tsp tartaric acid
- 1-2 tsp ground ginger

U sing a potato peeler, remove the rind from the lemon in large pieces before squeezing all the juice. Put the sugar in a bowl and pour on the boiling water. Add the lemon juice and rind, the tartaric acid and the ginger. Stir to dissolve the sugar, cover with a tea towel and leave until cold.

Serve in long glasses with lime wedges and a few ice cubes. Remove the lemon rind, add the very cold water and serve.

CORNISH MAHOGANY

serves 6

- 2 cups of gin
- 1 cup of treacle

B eat the ingredients together and serve immediately. You could substitute treacle for golden syrup.

This works well and has a lighter flavour than treacle. Either way, it's not a drink for children.

ST AGNES MULLED WINE
serves 6

- 75cl Shiraz
- 150ml orange juice
- 50g sugar
- 2 sprigs fresh rosemary
- 2 parcels of mulled wine spices & herbs
- 1 lemon
- 1 orange

To serve
- 10 mint leaves
- lemon & orange slices – cut in half
- 2 cinnamon sticks per glass
- 2 redcurrants per glass

Cut the lemon and orange in half before slicing across. Combine the ingredients in a pan over a gentle heat until the sugar has dissolved. Increase the heat until a mild simmer appears around the edges of the wine. Leave to simmer for 8 minutes before turning the heat down.

Place 4 half slices of lemon and orange and a mint leaf in the bottom of each glass and pour over the mulled wine. Push the cinnamon sticks into the glass, top with the redcurrants and serve.

Note: this recipe may be multiplied although three bottles of wine is usually the optimum number in any one preparation.